Geometry
Quick Starts

Author: Vicky Shiotsu
Editor: Mary Dieterich
Proofreaders: Margaret Brown and April Albert

COPYRIGHT © 2019 Mark Twain Media, Inc.

ISBN 978-1-62223-772-2

Printing No. CD-405038

Mark Twain Media, Inc., Publishers
Distributed by Carson-Dellosa Publishing LLC

Table of Contents

Introduction to the Teacher

The activities presented in *Geometry Quick Starts* provide teachers and parents with activities to help students develop and reinforce geometry-related skills. These quick activities help students prepare for the day's lesson while reviewing what they have previously learned. Each page contains two to four quick starts. Used at the beginning of class, quick starts help students focus on geometry-related concepts.

Geometry is the branch of mathematics that deals with the measurement, properties, and relationships of points, lines, angles, surfaces, and solids. The quick start activities in this book move from the most basic lines to more complex concepts such as angles, polygons, symmetry, transformations, perimeter, area, volume, circles, solid figures, and the coordinate plane.

Although the quick starts have been arranged to present more basic topics up front, you do not need to give them to your class in sequential order. Choose the pages in the order that best fits your curriculum needs. In addition, the activities that are on the same page may be presented in any order.

Suggestions for use:

- Copy and cut apart a page of quick starts. Give students one or more activities each day at the beginning of class.

- Give each student a copy of the entire page to complete day by day. Students can keep the completed pages in a three-ring binder or folder to use as a resource.

- Make transparencies of individual quick starts and complete the activities as a group.

- Provide additional copies of quick starts in your learning center for students to complete at random when they have a few extra minutes.

- Keep some quick starts on hand to use as fill-ins when the class has a few extra minutes before lunch or dismissal.

Lines, Rays, Line Segments, and Angles

Lines, Rays, and Line Segments 1

Label each figure as a **line**, **ray**, or **line segment**.

A. ●———● _____

B. ◄———► _____

C. ●———► _____

D. ◄———● _____

Lines, Rays, and Line Segments 2

How many line segments are in the picture? _____

Name them.

_____

_____

_____

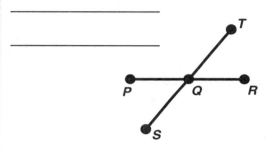

Lines, Rays, and Line Segments 3

Use letters and symbols to label each figure.

This line is $\overleftrightarrow{AB}$ or $\overleftrightarrow{BA}$.

A. G   H   _____

B. R   S   _____

C. U   V   _____

Lines, Rays, and Line Segments 4

Are the following statements true or false?

A. A line segment has only one endpoint. _____

B. A line has two endpoints. _____

C. A ray goes on without end in one direction. _____

D. A line goes on without end in two directions. _____

Lines, Rays, Line Segments, and Angles

Lines, Rays, and Line Segments 5

Look at the picture. Name the following figures.

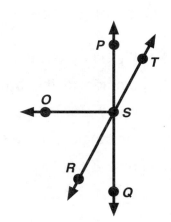

A. two lines _____

B. five rays _____

C. two line segments that contain point Q

_____

Classifying Angles 1

Write three names for each angle. Use symbols and letters.
(Examples: ∠PQR, ∠RQP, ∠Q)

A.

B.

C.

_____   _____   _____

_____   _____   _____

_____   _____   _____

Classifying Angles 2

Write **acute**, **obtuse**, **right**, or **straight** to describe the angles.

A.

B.

C.

D.

_____   _____   _____   _____

Lines, Rays, Line Segments, and Angles

Classifying Angles 3

A. What do you call the point that is common to the two sides of an angle? _____

B. Can angle *XYZ* also be named angle *ZYX*? Explain. _____

_____

_____

C. Can angle *XYZ* also be called angle *YZX*? Explain. _____

_____

_____

Classifying Angles 4

Write **acute**, **obtuse**, **right**, or **straight** to answer each question.

A. Which angle measures 90 degrees? _____

B. Which angle is greater than 90 degrees but less than 180 degrees? _____

C. Which angle is less than 90 degrees? _____

D. Which angle equals 180 degrees? _____

Classifying Angles 5

Use the figure at right to complete the exercises.

A. Name an acute angle. _____

B. Name a right angle. _____

C. Name a straight angle. _____

D. Name an obtuse angle. _____

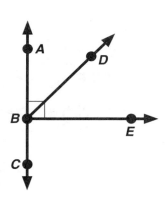

Lines, Rays, Line Segments, and Angles

Measuring and Drawing Angles 1

Write the missing numbers.

A. A straight angle measures

_____ degrees.

B. A right angle measures

_____ degrees.

C. An acute angle measures less

than _____ degrees but greater

than _____ degrees.

D. An obtuse angle measures greater

than _____ degrees but less than

_____ degrees.

Measuring and Drawing Angles 2

Use a protractor to measure the angles.

A. _____°

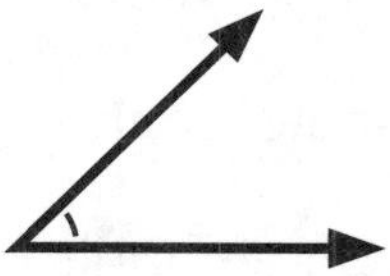

B. _____°

C. _____°

Measuring and Drawing Angles 3

Use a protractor to draw the angles with the following measures.

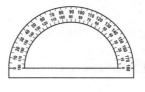

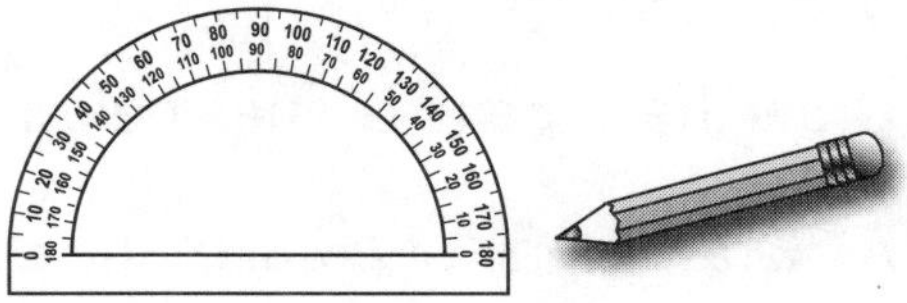

A. 30°   B. 60°   C. 135°   D. 90°

Lines, Rays, Line Segments, and Angles

Measuring and Drawing Angles 4

Draw the following angles on a separate sheet of paper. Then use a protractor to measure your angles.

A. an acute angle

B. an obtuse angle

C. a right angle

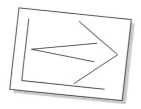

Measuring and Drawing Angles 5

Use a protractor to measure angles *A, B, C*, and *D*. Write **acute**, **obtuse**, or **right** beside each measure.

A. _____

B. _____

C. _____

D. _____

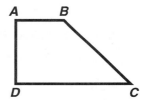

Classifying Pairs of Lines 1

Draw these pairs of lines below.

A. Draw a pair of parallel lines.

B. Draw a pair of perpendicular lines.

C. Draw a pair of intersecting lines that are not perpendicular.

Classifying Pairs of Lines 2

Write *T* for true or *F* for false.

_____ A. Parallel lines never intersect.

_____ B. Some intersecting lines are perpendicular.

_____ C. Perpendicular lines rarely intersect.

_____ D. If two lines are perpendicular, then they are also parallel.

Lines, Rays, Line Segments, and Angles

Classifying Pairs of Lines 3

A. Name two parallel lines.

_____

B. Name two perpendicular lines.

_____

C. Name two intersecting lines

that are not perpendicular.

_____

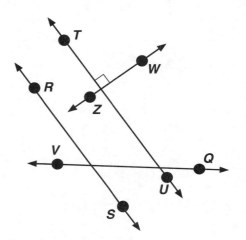

Classifying Pairs of Lines 4

Write **parallel**, **perpendicular**, or **intersecting** for each pair of lines.

A. $\overleftrightarrow{RU}$ and $\overleftrightarrow{TV}$ _____

B. $\overleftrightarrow{SQ}$ and $\overleftrightarrow{RU}$ _____

C. $\overleftrightarrow{RT}$ and $\overleftrightarrow{RU}$ _____

D. $\overleftrightarrow{UV}$ and $\overleftrightarrow{SQ}$ _____

E. $\overleftrightarrow{TV}$ and $\overleftrightarrow{QS}$ _____

F. $\overleftrightarrow{VT}$ and $\overleftrightarrow{TR}$ _____

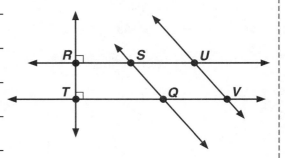

Lines, Rays, Line Segments, and Angles

Classifying Pairs of Lines 5

Write **parallel**, **perpendicular**, or **intersecting** to describe each set of lines.

A. _____

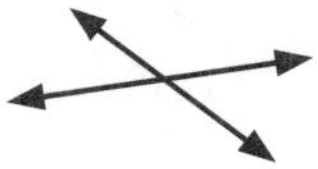

B. _____

C. _____

D. _____

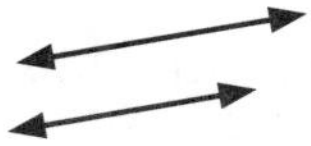

Special Pairs of Angles 1

Write **vertical**, **complementary**, or **supplementary** to describe each pair of angles.

A. The sum of the measures of these two angles is 180 degrees.

_____

B. These angles are always congruent.

_____

C. The sum of the measures of these two angles is 90 degrees.

_____

Special Pairs of Angles 2

The angles in each pair are complementary. Write the missing angle measures.

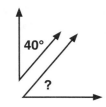

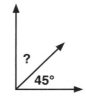

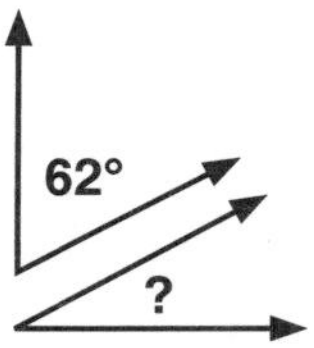

A. _____°

B. _____°

C. _____°

Lines, Rays, Line Segments, and Angles

Special Pairs of Angles 3

The angles in each pair are supplementary. Write the missing angle measures.

A. _____°

B. _____°

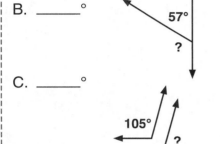

C. _____°

Special Pairs of Angles 4

A. Two angles are vertical. One angle measures 112 degrees. The other measures _____ degrees.

B. Two angles are supplementary. One measures 97 degrees. The other measures _____ degrees.

C. Two angles are complementary. One angle measures 36 degrees. The other measures _____ degrees.

Special Pairs of Angles 5

A. Two complementary angles have the same measure.

What is their angle measure? _____

B. Two supplementary angles have the same measure.

What is their angle measure? _____

C. Two angles are complementary. One angle is twice the other.

What are the angle measures? _____

D. Two angles are supplementary. One angle measures 10 degrees more than

the other. What are the angle measures? _____

Polygons

Identifying Polygons 1

Are these figures polygons?

A. _____

B. _____

C. _____

D. _____

E. _____

F. _____

Identifying Polygons 2

How many sides, angles, and vertices do these polygons have?

	Sides	Angles	Vertices
A. pentagon	_____	_____	_____
B. quadrilateral	_____	_____	_____
C. octagon	_____	_____	_____
D. hexagon	_____	_____	_____

Identifying Polygons 3

Write the names of these polygons.

 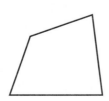 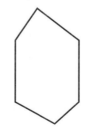 

A. _____   B. _____   C. _____   D. _____

Polygons

Identifying Polygons 4

A. Can a polygon have only two

   vertices? _____

   Explain. _____

   _____

   _____

B. Is a circle a polygon? _____

   Explain. _____

   _____

   _____

Identifying Polygons 5

A. Are all rectangles squares? _____

   Explain. _____

   _____

   _____

   _____

B. Are all squares rectangles? _____

   Explain. _____

   _____

   _____

   _____

Polygon Puzzles 1

A. Draw two squares using only five
   lines.

B. Draw two squares using only six
   lines.

Polygon Puzzles 2

A. Draw two triangles that are the
   same size and shape using only
   four lines.

B. Draw two triangles that are the
   same size and shape using only
   five lines.

Polygons

Polygon Puzzles 3

Suppose you were going to cut this rectangle in half along the lines.

How many different ways could you cut it? _____

Draw your answers in the space below.

Polygon Puzzles 4

How many triangles are in this figure?

_____

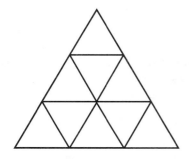

Polygon Puzzles 5

A. Draw two lines to divide the shape into three equal parts.

B. Connect the dots so that you get two squares.

Properties of Geometric Figures

Congruent Figures 1

Two figures are **congruent** if they are exactly equal in size and shape.

Are the two figures in each set congruent?

A.

B.

C.

D.

_____   _____   _____   _____

Congruent Figures 2

Which two figures in each row are congruent? Write the numbers on the lines.

A. _____

B. _____

C. _____

Congruent Figures 3

Triangle *ABC* is congruent to triangle *DEF*.

A. Which segment is congruent to $\overline{AB}$? _____

B. Which segment is congruent to $\overline{BC}$? _____

C. Which segment is congruent to $\overline{AC}$? _____

D. Which angle is congruent to $\angle ABC$? _____

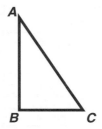
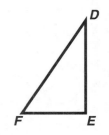

Properties of Geometric Figures

Congruent Figures 4

Draw the following figures.

A. Draw a triangle that has exactly two congruent sides.

B. Draw a triangle that has three congruent sides.

C. Draw a figure that has four sides. Make all the sides congruent. Do not make a square.

Congruent Figures 5

Use the square to do the following:

A. Name the triangles that are congruent to triangle *AXB*.

_____

B. Name the segments that are congruent to $\overline{AC}$.

_____

C. Which triangles are congruent to triangle *ADC*?

_____

Similar Figures 1

Two figures are **similar** when they have the same shape. They have corresponding proportional sides and corresponding equal angles. The size of the two shapes may be different.

Are the two figures in each set similar?

A. _____   B. _____

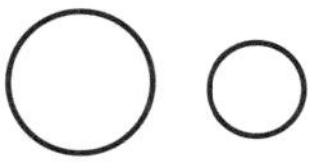

C. _____   D. _____

Similar Figures 2

Which two figures in each row are similar? Write the numbers.

A. _____

1.   2.   3.

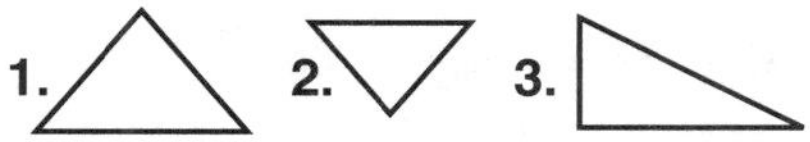

B. _____

4.   5.   6.

C. _____

7.   8.   9.

Properties of Geometric Figures

Similar Figures 3

Find the four pairs of similar figures. Write their numbers on the lines.

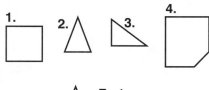

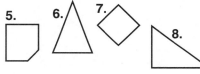

A. _____   B. _____

C. _____   D. _____

Similar Figures 4

Write *T* for true or *F* for false.

_____ A. All squares are similar.

_____ B. All rectangles are similar.

_____ C. All triangles are similar.

_____ D. All circles are similar.

_____ E. All hexagons are similar.

Similar Figures 5

The figures in each pair are similar. Find the missing lengths.

A. *s* = _____

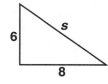

B. *t* = _____

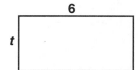

C. *x* = _____

y = _____

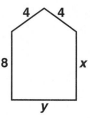

Properties of Geometric Figures

Symmetrical Figures 1

A **line of symmetry** divides a figure into two mirror-image halves. The figure can be folded over the line and match up exactly.

Is the dashed line a line of symmetry?

A. _____   B. _____   C. _____   D. _____

Symmetrical Figures 2

Is the letter symmetrical? Write "yes" or "no." If it is, draw the line of symmetry.

A. _____   B. _____   C. _____

D. _____   E. _____   F. _____

Symmetrical Figures 3

Draw a line of symmetry through each figure.

A.   B.   C.   D.   E.

              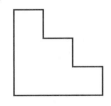

Properties of Geometric Figures

Symmetrical Figures 4

Write how many lines of symmetry each figure has. Then draw them.

A.

B.

_____   _____

C.

_____

Symmetrical Figures 5

Complete the missing half of each design to find the missing words.

A. OX

B. HOE

C. DID

D. ICE

Two Types of Symmetry 1

Does the figure have line symmetry? If it does, draw the line of symmetry.

A. _____

B. _____

C. _____

D. _____

Two Types of Symmetry 2

A figure has rotational symmetry if it can be rotated less than 360° around a central point and still match the original. Does the figure have rotational symmetry?

A.

B.

C. _____

D. _____

Properties of Geometric Figures

Two Types of Symmetry 3

Write **line**, **rotational**, or **both** to show what kind of symmetry each design has.

A. _____

B. _____

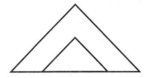

C. _____

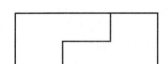

D. _____

Two Types of Symmetry 4

Look at each letter. Write **line**, **rotational**, or **both** to show what kind of symmetry it has.

A. _____

B. _____

C. _____

D. _____

Two Types of Symmetry 5

A. Draw a figure that has line symmetry.

B. Draw a figure that has rotational symmetry.

Properties of Geometric Figures

Transformations 1

A **reflection** flips a figure across a line. Draw the reflection of each figure below.

A.

B.

C.

Transformations 2

A **translation** slides a figure in a given direction. Draw the translation of each figure.

A.

B.

C.

Transformations 3

Write whether the transformation is a **reflection**, **translation**, or **rotation**.

A.

B.

C.

Transformations 4

List the capital letters of the alphabet that remain the same when they are reflected across a vertical line.

_____

_____

_____

_____

Properties of Geometric Figures

Transformations 5

A **rotation** turns a figure about a given point.

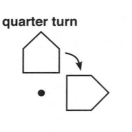

quarter turn   **half turn**   **three-quarters turn**

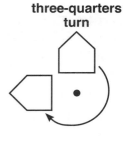

Draw a clockwise rotation of this figure:

A. a quarter turn

B. a half turn

C. a three-quarters turn

Geometric Patterns 1

Color the shapes to extend each pattern. Then make up your own pattern for the last picture.

A.

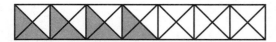

B.

C.

D.

Properties of Geometric Figures

Geometric Patterns 2

Draw the next two figures in each pattern.

A.

B.

C.

Geometric Patterns 3

How many squares are needed to make the seventh figure in the pattern below? _____

Describe how you found the answer.

_____

_____

_____

_____

Geometric Patterns 4

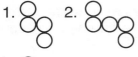 

How many circles are needed for the tenth figure in the pattern? _____

How can you find out without using counters or drawing a picture?

_____

_____

_____

Geometric Patterns 5

How many triangles are needed in all if you extend the pattern to eight rows? _____

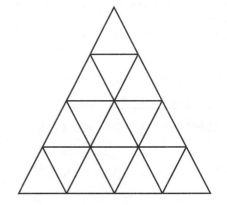

Classifying Geometric Figures

Classifying Triangles 1

Write **equilateral**, **isosceles**, or **scalene** to describe each triangle.

A. _____

B. _____

C. _____

Classifying Triangles 2

Write **acute**, **right**, or **obtuse** to describe each triangle.

A. _____

B. _____

C. _____

Classifying Triangles 3

Match the words with their clues. You will not use two of the words.

equilateral	**isosceles**
scalene	**right**
obtuse	**acute**

A. No sides are the same length.

_____

B. One angle is 90°.

_____

C. At least two sides are equal.

_____

D. All angles are less than 90°.

_____

Classifying Triangles 4

Write **A** for always, **S** for sometimes, or **N** for never on the line next to each statement.

____ A. A right triangle is a scalene triangle.

____ B. An equilateral triangle is an isosceles triangle.

____ C. An isosceles triangle is a right triangle.

____ D. An equilateral triangle is obtuse.

Classifying Geometric Figures

Classifying Triangles 5

equilateral	scalene
isosceles	right
obtuse	acute

Write two words from the box to describe each triangle.

A. 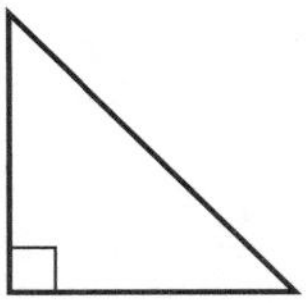 　　B. 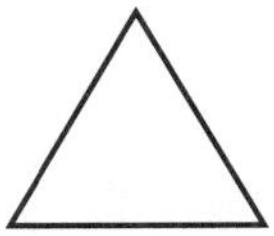 　　C.  　　D.

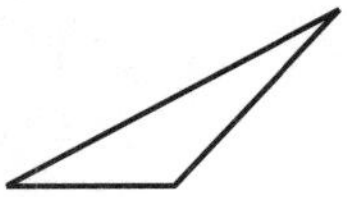

_____　　_____　　_____　　_____

_____　　_____　　_____　　_____

Classifying Quadrilaterals 1

For each name, write the numbers of all the shapes that apply.

A. rhombus _____

B. rectangle _____

C. trapezoid _____

D. parallelogram _____

E. quadrilateral _____

1.  　　2.

3. 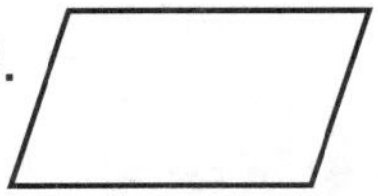　　4.

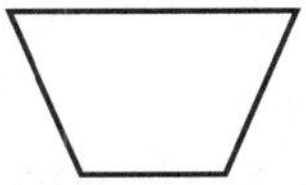

5. 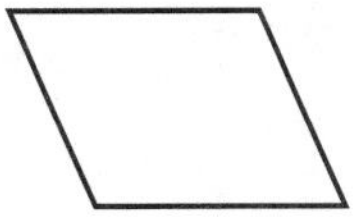　　6. 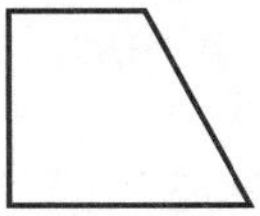　　7.

Classifying Quadrilaterals 2

Write the numbers of the figures that are trapezoids.

_____

1.  　　2. 　　3.  　　4.

5. 　　6.  　　7.  　　8.

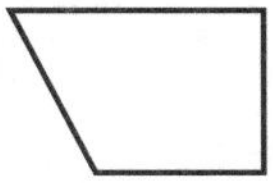

Classifying Geometric Figures

Classifying Quadrilaterals 3

Look at each figure. Is it a quadrilateral?

A. _____   B. _____

C. _____   D. _____

E. _____   F. _____

Classifying Quadrilaterals 4

A. Draw a quadrilateral with exactly one pair of parallel lines.

B. Draw a quadrilateral with four congruent sides.

C. Draw a quadrilateral with two pairs of parallel sides and four right angles.

Classifying Quadrilaterals 5

A. Are all squares rhombuses? _____

Explain. _____

_____

_____

B. Do all quadrilaterals have at least one pair of parallel sides?

_____

Explain. _____

_____

_____

Classifying Parallelograms 1

Write the names from the box that match each clue. The words will be used more than once.

| rhombus |
| rectangle |
| square |

A. has four congruent sides

_____

B. has four right angles

_____

C. has opposite sides that are congruent and parallel

_____

_____

Classifying Geometric Figures

Classifying Parallelograms 2

Look at each figure. Is it a parallelogram?

A. _____

B. _____

C. _____

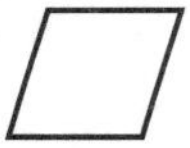

D. _____

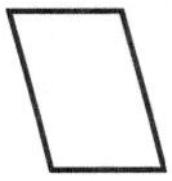

E. _____

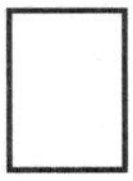

F. _____

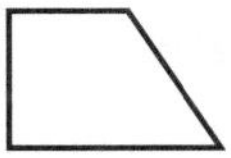

Classifying Parallelograms 3

A. Are all rectangles parallelograms?

_____

Explain. _____

_____

_____

B. Are all quadrilaterals

parallelograms? _____

Explain. _____

_____

_____

Classifying Parallelograms 4

The figure at the right is a parallelogram.

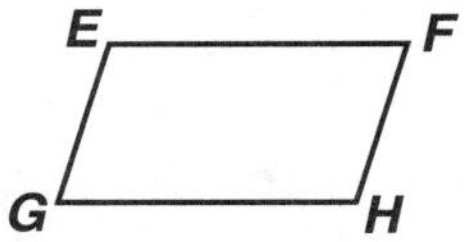

A. Which segments are congruent?

_____

_____

B. Which segments are parallel?

_____

_____

Classifying Parallelograms 5

Figure *QRST* is a parallelogram. Write the names of all the other parallelograms in the picture.

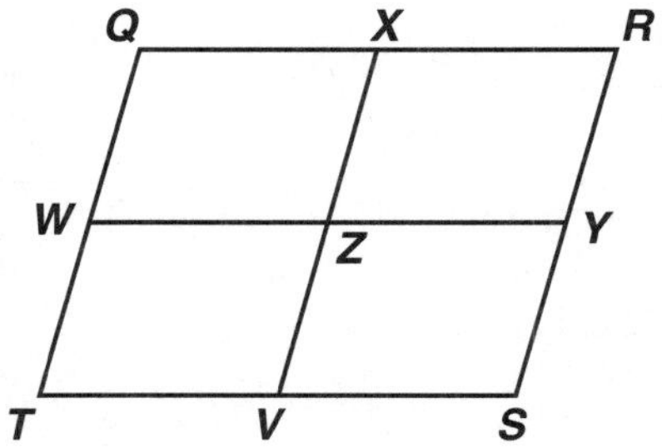

_____

_____

_____

Angle Measures of Geometric Figures

Angle Measures of Triangles 1

A. What is the sum of the angle measures of a triangle?

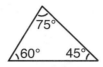

_____ degrees

B. Why can't a triangle have two right

angles? _____

_____

_____

_____

Angle Measures of Triangles 2

Triangle *ABC* is congruent to Triangle *DEF*.

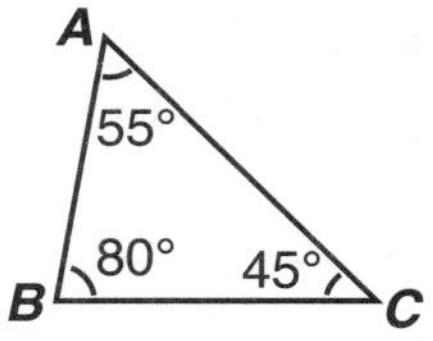

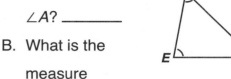

A. Which angle is

congruent to

∠*A*? _____

B. What is the

measure

of ∠*E*? _____

C. What is the measure

of ∠*F*? _____

Angle Measures of Triangles 3

Write the missing angle measures.

A. _____

B. _____

C. _____

D. _____

A.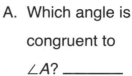

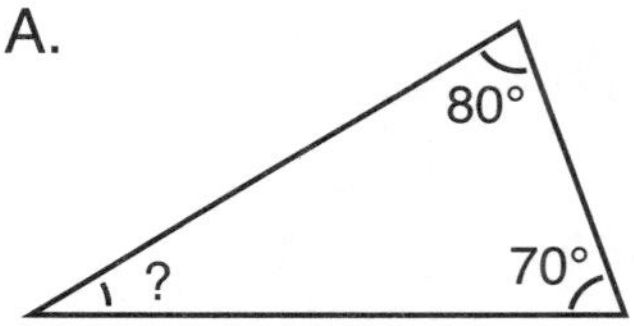

B.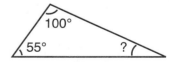

C.

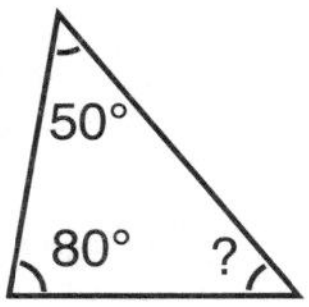

D.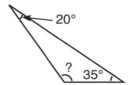

Angle Measures of Geometric Figures

Angle Measures of Triangles 4

The triangles below are right triangles. Write the missing angle measures.

A. _____

50°

B. _____

?
65°

C. _____

42°
?

D. _____

?
35°

Angle Measures of Triangles 5

A. In a right triangle, the two acute angles have the same measure.

   What is their measure? _____

B. In an equilateral triangle, all the angles have the same measure.

   What is it? _____

C. In a right triangle, one acute angle is twice the size of the other.

   What are their measures?

   _____

Angle Measures of Quadrilaterals 1

A. What is the sum of the angle measures of a quadrilateral?

120°   70°
60°   110°

   _____ degrees

B. Why can't a quadrilateral have more than three obtuse angles?

   _____

   _____

   _____

Angle Measures of Quadrilaterals 2

The opposite angles of a parallelogram are congruent.

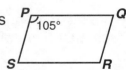
P   105°   Q
S   R

A. Which angle is congruent to ∠P?

   _____

B. What is the measure of ∠Q?

   _____

C. What is the sum of the measures

   of ∠P and ∠Q? _____

Angle Measures of Geometric Figures

Angle Measures of Quadrilaterals 3

Write the missing angle measures for each quadrilateral.

A. _____

B. _____

C. _____

D. _____

A.
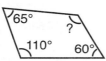

B.
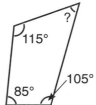

C.
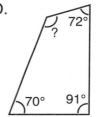

D.

Angle Measures of Quadrilaterals 4

Write the missing angle measures for each quadrilateral.

A. _____

B. _____

C. _____

D. _____

Angle Measures of Quadrilaterals 5

This figure is a parallelogram. The measure of ∠B is twice the measure of ∠A. What are the measures of the four angles?

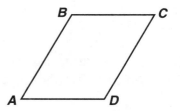

∠A = _____°   ∠B = _____°

∠C = _____°   ∠D = _____°

Perimeter

Perimeter of Rectangles and Squares 1

Find the perimeter of each figure.

A. _____ m

2 m
3 m

B. _____ in.

6 in.
6 in.

C. _____ ft.

3 ft.
1 ft.

Perimeter of Rectangles and Squares 2

A. A square has sides that are 7 feet long. What is its perimeter?

_____

B. A rectangle is 12 inches long and 10 inches wide. What is its perimeter?

_____

C. A rectangle is twice as long as it is wide. The rectangle is 8 meters wide. What is its perimeter?

_____

Perimeter of Rectangles and Squares 3

A. The perimeter of a square is 12 cm. What is the length of each side?

_____

B. The perimeter of a rectangle is 24 ft. The rectangle is 8 ft. long. What is its width?

_____

C. The perimeter of a rectangle is 32 m. Its length is 6 m longer than its width. What are the length and width?

_____

Perimeter of Rectangles and Squares 4

A. A square has sides that are 6 ft. long. What is its perimeter in feet? What is it in yards?

6 ft.
6 ft.

_____

B. A rectangle is 24 in. x 48 in. What is its perimeter in inches? What is it in feet?

24 in.
48 in.

_____

Perimeter

Perimeter of Rectangles and Squares 5

A rectangle has a perimeter of 14 inches. The length of each side is a whole number in inches. Draw the possible rectangles with their measurements labeled.

Perimeter of Polygons 1

Find the perimeter of each triangle.

A.

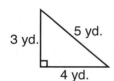

3 yd.   5 yd.

4 yd.

_____ yd.

B.

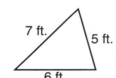

7 ft.   5 ft.

6 ft.

_____ ft.

C.

10 cm   10 cm

8 cm

_____ cm

Perimeter of Polygons 2

A regular polygon has sides of equal lengths. Find the perimeter of each regular polygon below.

A.

6 m

_____ m

B.

12 cm

_____ cm

C.

9 in.

_____ in.

Perimeter

Perimeter of Polygons 3

Find the perimeter of each figure in both inches and feet.

A.

6 in.
9 in. / 9 in.
12 in.

B.

7 in.
4 in.   3 in.
7 in.   3 in.

C.

3 ft.
9 ft.   9 ft.
3 ft.

Perimeter = ____ in.   Perimeter = ____ in.   Perimeter = ____ in.

Perimeter = ____ ft.   Perimeter = ____ ft.   Perimeter = ____ ft.

Perimeter of Polygons 4

A. An equilateral triangle has a perimeter of 18 cm. What is the length of each side?

_____

B. A regular pentagon has a perimeter of 45 ft. What is the length of each side?

_____

C. A rhombus has a perimeter of 28 m. What is the length of each side?

_____

Perimeter of Polygons 5

The figures are regular polygons. Write their number(s) to answer the questions.

A. Which figure has the greatest perimeter? ____

B. Which figure has the least perimeter? ____

C. Which figures have the same perimeter? ____

1.   8 in.   2.   7 in.

3.   5 in.   4.

12 in.

Perimeter

Perimeter of Complex Figures 1

Find the perimeter of each figure.

A. _____ yd.

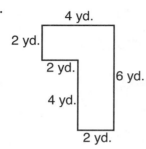

B. _____ cm

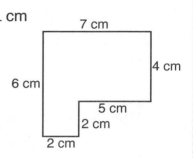

Perimeter of Complex Figures 2

Find the perimeter of each figure.

A. _____ m

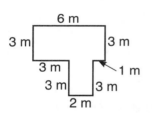

B. _____ in.

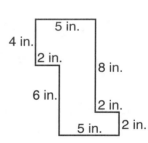

Perimeter of Complex Figures 3

The diagram shows the shape of Lee's garden. Lee will put a fence around the garden. Fencing costs $2.00 per foot.

A. How many feet of fencing will Lee need?

_____

B. How much will the fencing cost?

_____

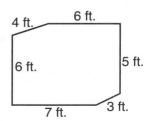

Perimeter

Perimeter of Complex Figures 4

Find the missing measures. Then find the perimeter.

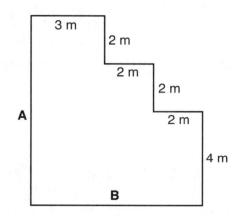

A = _____ m

B = _____ m

Perimeter = _____ m

Perimeter of Complex Figures 5

Find the missing measures. Then find the perimeter of each figure.

A = _____ m Perimeter = _____ m

B = _____ in. Perimeter = _____ in.

C = _____ ft. Perimeter = _____ ft.

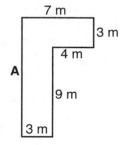
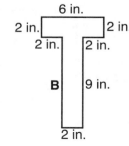
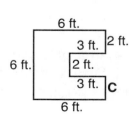

Area

Area of Rectangles and Squares 1

Find the area of each figure.

A. _____ in.²   B. _____ cm²

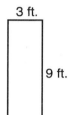

8 in.

12 in.

7 cm

C. _____ ft.²   3 ft.

9 ft.

Area of Rectangles and Squares 2

A. Anna is getting a new carpet for her room. The floor is 12 feet wide and 15 feet long. How many square feet of carpeting will she need?

_____

B. The area of a rectangular rug is 760 square inches. The width of the rug is 20 inches. What is its length?

_____

Area of Rectangles and Squares 3

A. The side of a square measures 6 inches. What is the area of the square?

_____

B. The area of a square is 121 square centimeters. What is the length of each side?

_____

C. The area of a square is 9 square feet. What is its area measured in square yards?

_____

Area of Rectangles and Squares 4

A. A rectangle has a perimeter of 24 meters and an area of 32 square meters. What are the lengths of its sides?

_____

_____

B. The perimeter of a square is 28 inches. What is its area?

_____

Area

Area of Rectangles and Squares 5

This rectangle has a perimeter of 12 units. Draw two other rectangles with a perimeter of 12 units. (Use only whole numbers for the lengths of the sides.)

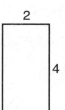

2

4

Which of the rectangles has the greatest area?

_____

Area of Triangles 1

Find the area of each triangle.

A. _____   B. _____   C. _____

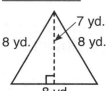

8 yd.   7 yd.   8 yd.

8 yd.

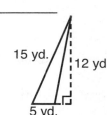

15 yd.   12 yd.

5 yd.

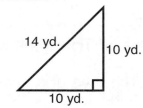

14 yd.   10 yd.

10 yd.

D. Which triangle has the greatest area—A, B, or C? _____

Area of Triangles 2

The area of this triangle can be expressed as $\frac{1}{2}ba$.

Write an expression for the areas below.

c   a   d

b

A.

r   u
t
s

_____

B.

z   y

x

_____

Area

Area of Triangles 3

Find the area of each triangle.

A. _____ in.²

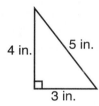

4 in.   5 in.

3 in.

B. _____ ft.²

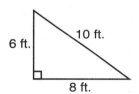

6 ft.   10 ft.

8 ft.

Area of Triangles 4

Find the area of each triangle.

A. _____ yd.²

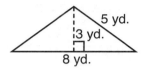

5 yd.

3 yd.

8 yd.

B. _____ cm²

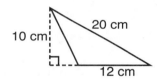

10 cm   20 cm

12 cm

Area of Triangles 5

A. The area of a triangle is 60 cm². If the height is 15 cm, what is the length of the base?

_____

B. The area of a triangle is 54 ft.². If the base is 9 ft., what is the height of the triangle?

_____

Area of Parallelograms 1

Find the area.

A. _____ m²

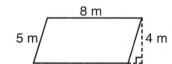

8 m

5 m   4 m

B. _____ cm²

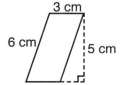

3 cm

6 cm   5 cm

Area

Area of Parallelograms 2

Find the area.

A. _____ ft.^{2}

B. _____ m^2

C. _____ yd.^{2}

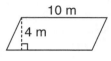

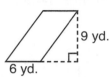

Area of Parallelograms 3

Find the area.

A.   B.   C.

A. _____ m^2

B. _____ m^2

C. _____ m^2

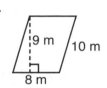

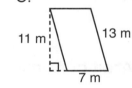

D. Which parallelogram has the greatest area? _____

E. Which one has the least area? _____

Area of Parallelograms 4

A. A parallelogram has an area of 42 cm. It is 7 cm high.

How long is the base? _____

B. A parallelogram has a base that is 12 in. long and a height of 7 in.

What is its area? _____

C. A parallelogram has an area of 143 ft.^{2}. Its base is 11 ft. long.

What is its height? _____

Area

Area of Complex Figures 1

Draw a line to divide each complex figure into two simple figures. Then find the area of the complex figure.

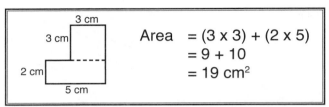

Area = (3 x 3) + (2 x 5)
       = 9 + 10
       = 19 cm²

A.

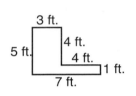

B.

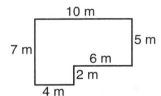

C.

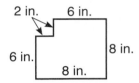

A. _____ ft.²

B. _____ m²

C. _____ in.²

Area of Complex Figures 2

Find the area of the figure.

Area = _____ m²

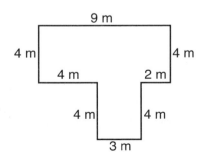

Area of Complex Figures 3

Find the value of x and y. Then find the area of the figure.

x = _____ ft.

y = _____ ft.

Area = _____ ft.²

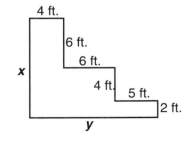

Area

Area of Complex Figures 4

Find the value of *x* and *y*. Then find the perimeter and area of the figure.

x = _____ yd.

y = _____ yd.

P = _____ yd.

A = _____ yd.²

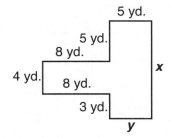

Area of Complex Figures 5

Find the value of *x* and *y*. Then find the perimeter and area of the figure.

x = _____ in.

y = _____ in.

P = _____ in.

A = _____ in.²

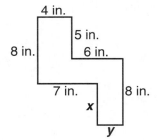

Area of Irregular Regions 1

Estimate the area of each irregular region in square units. First count each whole square that is covered. Then count each partial square as half a square. Add that amount to the number of whole squares.

This shape covers 2 whole squares and 10 partial ones. The total area is 7 square units (2 whole squares and 10 half-squares).

A. _____ square units

B. _____ square units

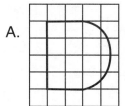

A.

B.

Area

Area of Irregular Regions 2

Estimate the number of square units in the region shown below.

_____ square units

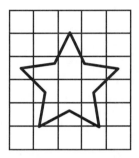

Area of Irregular Regions 3

Estimate the number of square units in the region shown below.

_____ square units

Area of Irregular Regions 4

Draw an irregular shape on the grid below. Estimate its area.

A = _____ square units

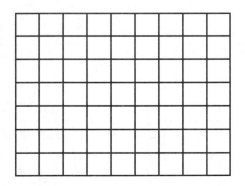

Area of Irregular Regions 5

Trace your hand on a sheet of graph paper. Count the squares to determine its area.

Circles

Circles 1

Write the word that matches each figure. Use the words in the box.

radius	center
diameter	chord

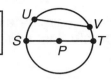

A. Point _P_ _____

B. $\overline{PT}$ _____

C. $\overline{UV}$ _____

D. $\overline{ST}$ _____

Circles 2

Draw a circle that contains the following:

A. center _M_

B. diameter $\overline{NS}$

C. radius $\overline{MP}$

D. chord $\overline{ST}$

Circles 3

Name the following:

A. two diameters _____

B. center of the circle _____

C. one chord _____

D. four radii _____

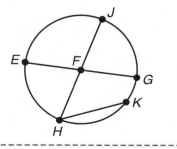

Circles 4

Write the correct word from the box for each definition below.

chord
diameter
radius
semicircle

A. Has one endpoint on a circle and the other endpoint at the center _____

B. Has both endpoints on a circle _____

C. Half a circle _____

D. Passes through the center of a circle and has both endpoints on the circle _____

Circles

Circles 5

A. $\overline{JK}$ is a radius of circle K. What is its length? _____

B. $\overline{KL}$ is a radius of circle K. What is its length? _____

C. How long is the diameter of circle K? _____

D. If you know the radius of a circle, how can you figure out the diameter? _____ _____

Circles and Central Angles 1

A **central angle** is an angle that has its vertex at the center of a circle.

In the circle below, ∠ABC is a central angle. List two other central angles.

_____   _____

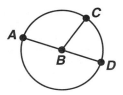

Circles and Central Angles 2

There are 360° in a circle.

A. What is the measure of ∠PQR?

_____

B. What is the measure of ∠PQS?

_____

C. What is the measure of ∠SQR?

_____

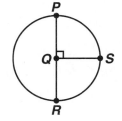

Circles and Central Angles 3

Draw the following features and label them on your diagram.

A. center L

B. radius $\overline{LM}$

C. chord $\overline{SM}$

D. central angle ∠XLY

E. central angle ∠XLZ

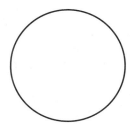

Circles

Circles and Central Angles 4

Write "**A**" if the statement is always true, "**S**" if it is sometimes true, and "**N**" if it is never true.

A. A central angle is greater than 90 degrees. _____

B. A central angle is formed by two radii of a circle. _____

C. A chord can be part of a central angle. _____

D. A diameter of a circle can form a central angle. _____

Circles and Central Angles 5

A. Draw two diameters on the first circle so that they form four central angles measuring 90°.

B. Draw two diameters on the second circle so that they form two obtuse central angles and two acute central angles.

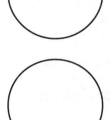

Circumference 1

Find the circumference. Use 3.14 for π and express the answer as a decimal. Or use $\frac{22}{7}$ for π and express the answer as a fraction in simplest form.

A. _____

B. _____

C. _____

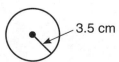
3.5 cm

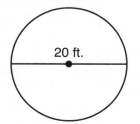
20 ft.

6 in.

Circles

Circumference 2

Fill in the blanks. You will not use all the answers provided.

| area |
| perimeter |
| three |
| five |
| π x *d* |
| π x *r* |

A. The circumference is

the _____

of a circle.

B. The circumference is about

_____ times greater than

the diameter.

C. The formula for finding

circumference is _____.

Circumference 3

Find the circumference. Use $\frac{22}{7}$ for π.

A. _____ in.

7 in.

B. _____ yd.

21 yd.

Circumference 4

Find the circumference. Use 3.14 for π.

A. _____ cm

4 cm

B. _____ m

5 m

Circumference 5

Use 3.14 for π to solve the problems.

A. The diameter of a circle is 8 cm.

What is the circumference?

_____

B. The radius of a circle is 2.5 ft.

What is the circumference?

_____

C. The circumference of a circle is

28.26 in.

What is the diameter?

_____

Circles

Area of Circles 1

The formula for finding the area of a circle using radius (r) is $\pi \times r \times r$, or πr^2.

Find each area. Use 3.14 for π.

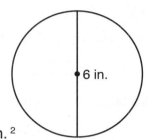

A. _____ cm²   B. _____ in.²

Area of Circles 2

Find each area. Use $\frac{22}{7}$ for π. Express the answer as a fraction in simplest form.

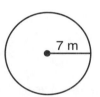   

A. _____ m²   B. _____ ft.²   C. _____ m²

Area of Circles 3

Use 3.14 for π to solve the problems.

A. The radius of a circle is 5 cm. What is the area? _____ cm²

B. The diameter of a circle is 40 yd. What is the area? _____ yd.²

C. The circumference of a circle is 62.8 m. How can you find the area?

_____

_____

_____

What is the area? _____ m²

Solid Figures

Solid Figures 1

A. Can a pyramid have a triangle for a base? _____

B. Can a pyramid have a square for a base? _____

C. Does a cylinder have any vertices? _____

D. Does a cone have any vertices? _____

E. Is a cube a rectangular prism? _____

Solid Figures 2

Write the number of faces, or flat surfaces, each figure has.

A. cube _____

B. cone _____

C. rectangular prism _____

D. square pyramid _____

E. cylinder _____

F. triangular prism _____

G. triangular pyramid _____

Solid Figures 3

Complete the table.

	Figure	Number of Edges	Number of Vertices
A.	Cube	12	
B.	Square Pyramid		
C.	Triangular Pyramid		
D.	Triangular Prism		
E.	Rectangular Prism		
F.	Pentagonal Prism		

Solid Figures 4

Are the statements true? Write "**A**" for always, "**S**" for sometimes, or "**N**" for never.

A. A pyramid has a square base. _____

B. The faces of a cube are congruent. _____

C. A regular cylinder has two circular faces that are congruent. _____

D. A sphere has a circular face. _____

Solid Figures

Solid Figures 5

Write the name of each figure.
Use the words in the box.
You will not use all the words.

| cube   cone   triangular prism   cylinder |
| triangular pyramid   square pyramid |
| rectangular prism   sphere |

A. _____

B. _____

C. _____

D. _____

A. 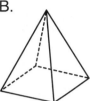 B. C. D.

Solid Figures and Nets 1

A **net** is a flat pattern that can be
folded to make a solid figure. Write the
name of the solid below its net. Use the
words in the box. (You will not use all the words.)

| cube   cone   triangular prism |
| triangular pyramid   square pyramid |
| rectangular prism |

        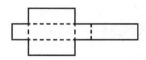

A. _____   B. _____   C. _____

Solid Figures and Nets 2

A **triangular pyramid** has four triangular faces.

Which diagram shows a net of a triangular pyramid? _____

A.   B.

Check your answer by first drawing larger copies of the patterns onto another
sheet of paper. Then cut them out and fold them.

Solid Figures

Solid Figures and Nets 3

Draw dashed lines to complete the nets.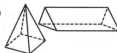

A. triangular prism

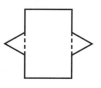

B. square pyramid

Solid Figures and Nets 4

A cube can have different nets. Draw two of the possible nets in the space below.

Surface Area of Rectangular Prisms 1

Use the net to find the surface area of the cube.

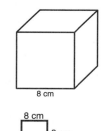

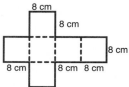

Surface Area = _____ cm²

Surface Area of Rectangular Prisms 2

A cube has sides measuring 5 inches.

What is the surface area of the cube?

_____

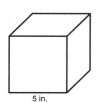

5 in.

Solid Figures

Surface Area of Rectangular Prisms 3

Use the net to find the surface area of the rectangular prism.

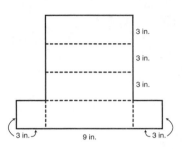

Surface Area = _____ in.²

Surface Area of Rectangular Prisms 4

Find the surface area of each figure.

A. Surface Area =

_____ m²

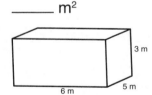

B. Surface Area =

_____ m²

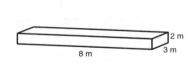

C. Surface Area =

_____ m²

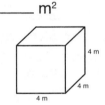

D. Which block has the greatest surface area? _____

Surface Area of Rectangular Prisms 5

Fill in the chart, and then answer the question.

Length of Side of Cube	Surface Area
1	
2	
4	
8	

What happens to the surface area when the sides of a cube are doubled?

_____

Solid Figures

Volume of Rectangular Prisms 1

Matt wants to fill this box with one-inch cubes. How many cubes will he need?

_____ cubes

How did you find the answer?

_____

_____

_____

_____

_____

Volume of Rectangular Prisms 2

Find the volume of each cube.

A.

3 in.

Volume = _____ in.^{3}

B.

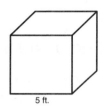

5 ft.

Volume = _____ ft.^{3}

Volume of Rectangular Prisms 3

Find the volume.

A.

7 cm

3 cm   1 cm

Volume = _____ cm^3

B.

10 m

8 m   4 m

Volume = _____ m^3

Volume of Rectangular Prisms 4

Kim wants to get the box with the greater volume.

Which box should she get—A or B?

_____

Box A:
length = 6 in.
width = 7 in.
height = 5 in.
Volume = _____ in.^{3}

Box B:
length = 8 in.
width = 6 in.
height = 4 in.
Volume = _____ in.^{3}

Solid Figures

Volume of Rectangular Prisms 5

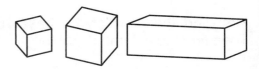

A. A cube has a volume of 216 cubic feet.
   What is the length of each side?

   _____

B. The volume of a rectangular prism is 128 cm³. The prism is 8 cm long and
   4 cm high. What is its width? _____

C. The surface area of a cube is 24 square inches. What is its volume?

   _____

Volume of Triangular Prisms 1

To find the volume of a triangular prism, first find the area
of the triangular base (B). Then multiply that by the prism's
height to find the volume (V).

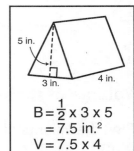

$B = \frac{1}{2} \times 3 \times 5$
$ = 7.5$ in.²
$V = 7.5 \times 4$
$ = 30$ in.³

A.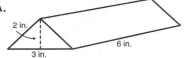

B = _____ in.²

V = _____ in.³

B.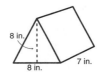

B = _____ in.²

V = _____ in.³

Volume of Triangular Prisms 2

A. A triangular prism has a base whose area is 14 in.². Its height is 5 inches.

   What is the volume of the prism? _____

B. A triangular prism has a volume of 54 cm³. Its height is 3 cm.

   What is the area of the triangular base? _____

Solid Figures

Volume of Triangular Prisms 3

First find the area of the base (B). Then find the volume (V) of the prism.

B = _____

V = _____

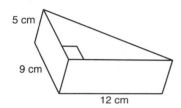

5 cm

9 cm

12 cm

Volume of Triangular Prisms 4

Which has the greater volume— A or B?

_____

A. V = _____

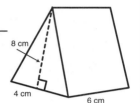

8 cm

4 cm

6 cm

B. V = _____

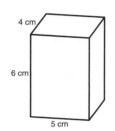

4 cm

6 cm

5 cm

Volume of Cylinders 1

Find the volume of each cylinder. First find the area of the circular base (B). Then multiply that by the height to find the volume (V).

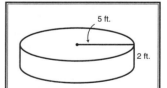

5 ft.

2 ft.

$B = \pi r^2$
$= 3.14 \times 5^2$
$= 78.5$ ft.^{2}

$V = 78.5 \times 2$
$= 157$ ft.^{3}

A.

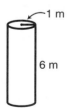

1 m

6 m

B.

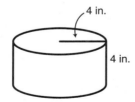

4 in.

4 in.

B = _____ m²

V = _____ m³

B = _____ in.²

V = _____ in.³

Solid Figures

Volume of Cylinders 2

Fill in the blanks with words from the box.

| area |
| cubic |
| circle |
| height |

A. A regular cylinder's base is a _____.

B. To find the _____ of the cylinder's base, use the formula πr^2.

C. To find the volume of a cylinder, multiply the area of the base by the _____.

D. Volume is measured in _____ units.

Volume of Cylinders 3

Which figure has the greater volume—A or B? _____

A. B = _____

   V = _____

B. B = _____

   V = _____

Volume of Cylinders 4

A. What is the volume of a cylinder that has a radius of 10 cm and a height of 10 cm?

   _____

B. What is the volume of a cylinder that has a radius of 5 cm and a height of 10 cm?

   _____

Volume of Cylinders 5

A. The volume of a cylinder is 141.3 yd.^{3}. The height of the cylinder is 5 yd. What is the area of the cylinder's base?

   _____

B. How did you solve the problem?

   _____

   _____

   _____

Coordinate Planes

Ordered Pairs 1

Write the letter for each ordered pair.

A. (2, 3) _____   B. (4, 5) _____

C. (6, 4) _____   D. (1, 5) _____

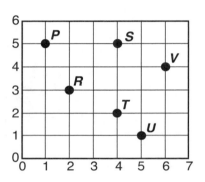

Ordered Pairs 2

Write the ordered pair for each point.

A _____   B _____

C _____   D _____

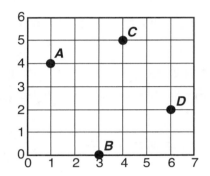

Ordered Pairs 3

Write the letter for each ordered pair.

A. (2, -3) _____   B. (-1, 3) _____

C. (-2, -2) _____   D. (3, 2) _____

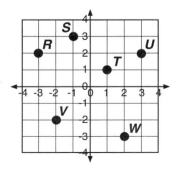

Ordered Pairs 4

Write the ordered pair for each point.

A _____   B _____

C _____   D _____

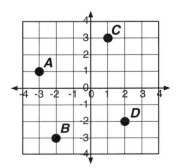

Coordinate Planes

Lengths on the Coordinate Plane 1

To find the length of a horizontal line segment, find the difference of the *x*-coordinates.

$\overline{AB}$ is _____ units long. A (**1**, 5) B (**4**, 5)

$4 - 1 = 3$

$\overline{CD}$ is _____ units long.

$\overline{EF}$ is _____ units long.

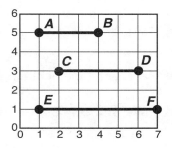

Lengths on the Coordinate Plane 2

To find the length of a vertical line segment, find the difference of the *y*-coordinates.

$\overline{JK}$ is _____ units long. J (1, **5**) K (1, **1**)

$5 - 1 = 4$

$\overline{LM}$ is _____ units long.

$\overline{NO}$ is _____ units long.

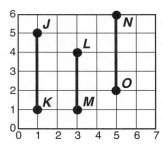

Lengths on the Coordinate Plane 3

Write the coordinates (ordered pairs) for each point.
Then find the lengths of the segments.

A _____ B _____ C _____

D _____ E _____ F _____

$\overline{AB}$ _____ units $\overline{CD}$ _____ units $\overline{DE}$ _____ units

$\overline{AF}$ _____ units $\overline{EF}$ _____ units $\overline{BC}$ _____ units

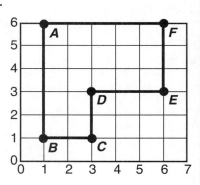

Answer Keys

Lines, Rays, and Line Segments 1 (p. 2)
A. line segment
B. line
C. ray
D. ray

Lines, Rays, and Line Segments 2 (p. 2)
A. 6: $\overline{PQ}, \overline{SQ}, \overline{QR}, \overline{QT}, \overline{PR}, \overline{ST}$
(or reverse order)

Lines, Rays, and Line Segments 3 (p. 2)
A. $\overleftrightarrow{GH}$ or $\overleftrightarrow{HG}$
B. $\overrightarrow{RS}$
C. $\overrightarrow{VU}$

Lines, Rays, and Line Segments 4 (p. 2)
A. false
B. false
C. true
D. true

Lines, Rays, and Line Segments 5 (p. 3)
A. $\overleftrightarrow{PQ}, \overleftrightarrow{TR}$ (or $\overleftrightarrow{QP}, \overleftrightarrow{RT}$)

B. $\overrightarrow{SQ}, \overrightarrow{SR}, \overrightarrow{ST}, \overrightarrow{SP}, \overrightarrow{SO}$

C. $\overline{QS}, \overline{QP}$ (or $\overline{SQ}, \overline{PQ}$)

Classifying Angles 1 (p. 3)
A. ∠LMN, ∠NML, ∠M
B. ∠GEH, ∠HEG, ∠E
C. ∠XVZ, ∠ZVX, ∠V

Classifying Angles 2 (p. 3)
A. acute
B. right
C. straight
D. obtuse

Classifying Angles 3 (p. 4)
A. vertex
B. Yes. Y is the vertex for both angles.
C. No. Angle YZX has point Z for a vertex rather than point Y.

Classifying Angles 4 (p. 4)
A. right
B. obtuse
C. acute
D. straight

Classifying Angles 5 (p. 4)
A. ∠ABD or ∠DBE
B. ∠ABE or ∠EBC
C. ∠ABC
D. ∠DBC

Measuring and Drawing Angles 1 (p. 5)
A. 180
B. 90
C. 90, 0
D. 90, 180

Measuring and Drawing Angles 2 (p. 5)
A. 45°
B. 100°
C. 120°

Measuring and Drawing Angles 3 (p. 5)
A. 30°
B. 60°
C. 135°
D. 90°

Measuring and Drawing Angles 4 (p. 6)
Angles and answers will vary.

Measuring and Drawing Angles 5 (p. 6)
A. 90°, right
B. 135°, obtuse
C. 45°, acute
D. 90°, right

Classifying Pairs of Lines 1 (p. 6)
Drawings should be made according to the directions.
Examples:

A. ↔ ↔
B. ⊥ (crossed lines with right angle)

C. X (two crossing lines)

Classifying Pairs of Lines 2 (p. 6)
A. T
B. T
C. F
D. F

Classifying Pairs of Lines 3 (p. 7)
A. $\overleftrightarrow{RS}, \overleftrightarrow{TU}$
B. $\overleftrightarrow{TU}, \overleftrightarrow{WZ}$
C. $\overleftrightarrow{RS}, \overleftrightarrow{VQ}$ or $\overleftrightarrow{TU}, \overleftrightarrow{VQ}$

Classifying Pairs of Lines 4 (p. 7)
A. parallel
B. intersecting
C. perpendicular
D. parallel
E. intersecting
F. perpendicular

Classifying Pairs of Lines 5 (p. 8)
A. intersecting
B. perpendicular
C. perpendicular
D. parallel

Special Pairs of Angles 1 (p. 8)
A. supplementary
B. vertical
C. complementary

Special Pairs of Angles 2 (p. 8)
A. 50°
B. 45°
C. 28°

Special Pairs of Angles 3 (p. 9)
A. 45°
B. 123°
C. 75°

Special Pairs of Angles 4 (p. 9)
A. 112   B. 83   C. 54

Special Pairs of Angles 5 (p. 9)
A. 45°   B. 90°   C. 60°, 30°
D. 95°, 85°

Identifying Polygons 1 (p. 10)
A. yes   B. no   C. yes   D. yes
E. yes   F. no

Identifying Polygons 2 (p. 10)
A. 5, 5, 5   B. 4, 4, 4   C. 8, 8, 8   D. 6, 6, 6

Identifying Polygons 3 (p. 10)
A. pentagon   B. quadrilateral
C. hexagon   D. octagon

Identifying Polygons 4 (p. 11)
A. No. A polygon needs at least 3 vertices to be a closed shape.
B. No. A circle is not made up of line segments.

Identifying Polygons 5 (p. 11)
A. No. A rectangle may have two pairs of sides that are different lengths.
B. Yes. A square is a special type of rectangle. All four sides are equal.

Polygon Puzzles 1 (p. 11)
A.   B.

Polygon Puzzles 2 (p. 11)
A.   B. or or

Polygon Puzzles 3 (p. 12)
There are 4 different ways to cut the rectangle in half.

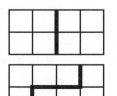

Polygon Puzzles 4 (p. 12)
There are 13 triangles: 9 small, one-cell triangles; 3 medium, four-cell triangles; and 1 large, nine-cell triangle.

Polygon Puzzles 5 (p. 12)
A.   B.

Congruent Figures 1 (p. 13)
A. no   B. no   C. yes   D. yes

Congruent Figures 2 (p. 13)
A. 1, 3   B. 5, 6   C. 7, 8

Congruent Figures 3 (p. 13)
A. $\overline{DE}$ B. $\overline{EF}$ C. $\overline{DF}$ D. $\angle DEF$

Congruent Figures 4 (p. 14)
Examples of drawings:
A.   B.   C.

Congruent Figures 5 (p. 14)
A. Triangles *BXC, CXD, DXA*   B. $\overline{BD}$ only
C. Triangles *DCB, CBA, BAD*

Similar Figures 1 (p. 14)
A. no   B. yes   C. yes   D. no

Similar Figures 2 (p. 14)
A. 1, 2   B. 4, 6   C. 7, 8

Similar Figures 3 (p. 15)
Pairs may be listed in any order.
A. 1, 7   B. 2, 6   C. 3, 8   D. 4, 5

Similar Figures 4 (p. 15)
A. T   B. F   C. F   D. T   E. F

Similar Figures 5 (p. 15)
A. $s = 10$ B. $t = 3$ C. $x = 8, y = 6$

Symmetrical Figures 1 (p. 16)
A. yes   B. no   C. yes   D. no

Symmetrical Figures 2 (p. 16)
A. yes   B. no   C. yes

D. no   E. yes   F. yes

Symmetrical Figures 3 (p. 16)

A.

B.

C.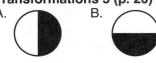

D.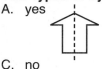

E.

Symmetrical Figures 4 (p. 17)

A. 2   B. 4   C. 3

Symmetrical Figures 5 (p. 17)

A. OX   B. HOE   C. DID   D. ICE

Two Types of Symmetry 1 (p. 17)

A. yes   B. no

C. no   D. yes

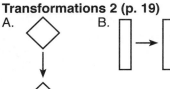

Two Types of Symmetry 2 (p. 17)

A. no   B. yes   C. yes   D. yes

Two Types of Symmetry 3 (p. 18)

A. both   B. line   C. rotational
D. both

Two Types of Symmetry 4 (p. 18)

A. line   B. both   C. rotational
D. line

Two Types of Symmetry 5 (p. 18)

A. Drawings will vary.   B. Drawings will vary.

Transformations 1 (p. 19)

A. **b**   B. [image]   C. [image]

Transformations 2 (p. 19)

A. [image]   B. [image]   C. [image]

Transformations 3 (p. 19)

A. translation   B. rotation   C. reflection

Transformations 4 (p. 19)

A, H, I, M, O, T, U, V, W, X, Y

Transformations 5 (p. 20)

A.   B.   C.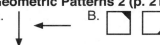

Geometric Patterns 1 (p. 20)

A.–C.   Teacher check patterns.
D.   Patterns will vary.

Geometric Patterns 2 (p. 21)

A. [image]   B. [image]   C. [image]

Geometric Patterns 3 (p. 21)

49; The first figure is a 1 x 1 square, the second is a 2 x 2 square, and so on. The 7th figure is made up of 7 x 7 (49) squares.

Geometric Patterns 4 (p. 21)

13; The number of counters used is 3 more than the number of the figure.

Geometric Patterns 5 (p. 21)

64; (1 + 3 + 5 + 7 + 9 + 11 + 13 + 15)

Classifying Triangles 1 (p. 22)

A. isosceles   B. equilateral   C. scalene

Classifying Triangles 2 (p. 22)

A. right   B. acute   C. obtuse

Classifying Triangles 3 (p. 22)

A. scalene   B. right   C. isosceles
D. acute

Classifying Triangles 4 (p. 22)

A. S   B. A   C. S   D. N

Classifying Triangles 5 (p. 23)

A. right, isosceles   B. acute, equilateral
C. right, scalene   D. obtuse, scalene

Classifying Quadrilaterals 1 (p. 23)

A. 5, 7   B. 2, 7   C. 4, 6
D. 2, 3, 5, 7   E. 1, 2, 3, 4, 5, 6, 7

Classifying Quadrilaterals 2 (p. 23)

2, 5, 7, 8

Classifying Quadrilaterals 3 (p. 24)

A. yes   B. no   C. yes   D. yes
E. no   F. yes

Classifying Quadrilaterals 4 (p. 24)
Teacher check drawings.
A. Drawing should be of a trapezoid.
B. Drawing should be of a rhombus or square.
C. Drawing should be of a rectangle or square.

Classifying Quadrilaterals 5 (p. 24)
A. Yes. A square is a rhombus that has four right angles.
B. No. Quadrilaterals have to have four sides, but the sides do not need to be parallel.

Classifying Parallelograms 1 (p. 24)
A. rhombus, square   B. rectangle, square
C. rhombus, rectangle, square

Classifying Parallelograms 2 (p. 25)
A. yes   B. no   C. yes   D. yes
E. yes   F. no

Classifying Parallelograms 3 (p. 25)
A. Yes. All rectangles have opposite sides that are congruent and parallel.
B. No. Some quadrilaterals have no parallel sides. Some have parallel sides that aren't congruent.

Classifying Parallelograms 4 (p. 25)

A. $\overline{EF}$ and $\overline{GH}$, $\overline{EG}$ and $\overline{FH}$

B. $\overline{EF}$ and $\overline{GH}$, $\overline{EG}$ and $\overline{FH}$

Classifying Parallelograms 5 (p. 25)
QXZW, XRYZ, WZVT, ZYSV, QXVT, XRSV, QRYW, WYST

Angle Measures of Triangles 1 (p. 26)
A. 180
B. If a triangle had two right angles, the sum of the three angle measures would be greater than 180 degrees.

Angle Measures of Triangles 2 (p. 26)
A. $\angle D$ B. 80°   C. 45°

Angle Measures of Triangles 3 (p. 26)
A. 30°   B. 25°   C. 50°   D. 125°

Angle Measures of Triangles 4 (p. 27)
A. 40°   B. 25°   C. 48°   D. 55°

Angle Measures of Triangles 5 (p. 27)
A. 45°   B. 60°   C. 60°, 30°

Angle Measures of Quadrilaterals 1 (p. 27)
A. 360
B. If it had more than three obtuse angles, the sum of the angle measures would be greater than 360 degrees.

Angle Measures of Quadrilaterals 2 (p. 27)
A. $\angle R$ B. 75°   C. 180°

Angle Measures of Quadrilaterals 3 (p. 28)
A. 80°   B. 55°   C. 125°   D. 127°

Angle Measures of Quadrilaterals 4 (p. 28)
A. 60°   B. 90°   C. 62°   D. 105°

Angle Measures of Quadrilaterals 5 (p. 28)
$\angle A = 60°$ $\angle B = 120°$ $\angle C = 60°$ $\angle D = 120°$

Perimeter of Rectangles and Squares 1 (p. 29)
A. 10   B. 24   C. 8

Perimeter of Rectangles and Squares 2 (p. 29)
A. 28 feet   B. 44 inches   C. 48 meters

Perimeter of Rectangles and Squares 3 (p. 29)
A. 3 cm   B. 4 ft.
C. length = 11 m; width = 5 m

Perimeter of Rectangles and Squares 4 (p. 29)
A. 24 ft., 8 yd.   B. 144 in., 12 ft.

Perimeter of Rectangles and Squares 5 (p. 30)
Teacher check rectangles.
Measurements should be:
3 in. by 4 in.;   2 in. by 5 in.;   6 in. by 1 in.

Perimeter of Polygons 1 (p. 30)
A. 12   B. 18   C. 28

Perimeter of Polygons 2 (p. 30)
A. 30   B. 48   C. 54

Perimeter of Polygons 3 (p. 31)
A. 36 in., 3 ft.   B. 24 in., 2 ft.
C. 288 in., 24 ft.

Perimeter of Polygons 4 (p. 31)
A. 6 cm   B. 9 ft.   C. 7 m

Perimeter of Polygons 5 (p. 31)
A. 2   B. 4   C. 1, 3

Perimeter of Complex Figures 1 (p. 32)
A. 20   B. 26

Perimeter of Complex Figures 2 (p. 32)
A. 24   B. 34

Perimeter of Complex Figures 3 (p. 32)
A. 31   B. $62.00

Perimeter of Complex Figures 4 (p. 33)
A = 8 m   B = 7 m   Perimeter = 30 m

Perimeter of Complex Figures 5 (p. 33)
A = 12 m; Perimeter = 38 m
B = 9 in.; Perimeter = 34 in.
C = 2 ft.; Perimeter = 30 ft.

Area of Rectangles and Squares 1 (p. 34)
A. 96   B. 49   C. 27

Area of Rectangles and Squares 2 (p. 34)
A. 180 ft.^{2} B. 38 in.

Area of Rectangles and Squares 3 (p. 34)
A. 36 in.^{2} B. 11 cm   C. 1 yd.^{2}

Area of Rectangles and Squares 4 (p. 34)
A. 8 meters, 4 meters B. 49 in.^{2}

Area of Rectangles and Squares 5 (p. 35)
Teacher check drawings. There should be a 3 x
3 square and a 5 x 1 rectangle.
The 3 x 3 square has the greatest area.

Area of Triangles 1 (p. 35)
A. 28 yd.^{2} B. 30 yd.^{2} C. 50 yd.^{2} D. C

Area of Triangles 2 (p. 35)
A. ½*su*   B. ½*xy*

Area of Triangles 3 (p. 36)
A. 6   B. 24

Area of Triangles 4 (p. 36)
A. 12   B. 60

Area of Triangles 5 (p. 36)
A. 8 cm   B. 12 ft.

Area of Parallelograms 1 (p. 36)
A. 32   B. 15

Area of Parallelograms 2 (p. 37)
A. 108   B. 40   C. 54

Area of Parallelograms 3 (p. 37)
A. 80   B. 72   C. 77   D. A
E. B

Area of Parallelograms 4 (p. 37)
A. 6 cm   B. 84 in.^{2} C. 13 ft.

Area of Complex Figures 1 (p. 38)
A. 19

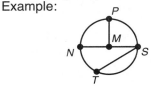

B. 58

C. 60

Area of Complex Figures 2 (p. 38)
48

Area of Complex Figures 3 (p. 38)
x = 12 ft.   *y* = 15 ft.   Area = 94 ft.^{2}

Area of Complex Figures 4 (p. 39)
x = 12 yd. *y* = 5 yd.   P = 50 yd.
A = 92 yd.^{2}

Area of Complex Figures 5 (p. 39)
x = 5 in.   *y* = 3 in.   P = 46 in.   A = 65 in.^{2}

Area of Irregular Regions 1 (p. 39)
A. 13 (10 whole squares and 6 half-squares)
B. 9 (6 whole squares and 6 half-squares)

Area of Irregular Regions 2 (p. 40)
7 (2 whole squares and 10 half-squares)

Area of Irregular Regions 3 (p. 40)
17.5 (9 whole squares and 17 half-squares)

Area of Irregular Regions 4 (p. 40)
Shape and area will vary.

Area of Irregular Regions 5 (p. 40)
Area will vary.

Circles 1 (p. 41)
A. center B. radius C. chord
D. diameter

Circles 2 (p. 41)
Example:

Circles 3 (p. 41)
A. $\overline{EG}$, $\overline{HJ}$ B. point *F*
C. $\overline{HK}$ D. $\overline{EF}$, $\overline{FG}$, $\overline{HF}$, $\overline{FJ}$

Circles 4 (p. 41)
A. radius   B. chord (also diameter)
C. semicircle   D. diameter

Circles 5 (p. 42)
A.   3 cm   B.   3 cm   C.   6 cm
D.   Multiply the length of the radius by 2.

Circles and Central Angles 1 (p. 42)
A. $\angle CBD$ B. $\angle ABD$

Circles and Central Angles 2 (p. 42)
A.   180°   B.   90°   C.   90°

Circles and Central Angles 3 (p. 42)
Example:

Circles and Central Angles 4 (p. 43)
A.   S   B.   A   C.   N   D.   A

Circles and Central Angles 5 (p. 43)
A.

B.

Circumference 1 (p. 43)
A.   21.98 cm or 22 cm   B.   62.8 ft. or $62\frac{6}{7}$ ft.
C.   37.68 in. or $37\frac{5}{7}$ in.

Circumference 2 (p. 44)
A.   perimeter   B.   three   C. $\pi \times d$

Circumference 3 (p. 44)
A.   44   B.   66

Circumference 4 (p. 44)
A.   12.56   B.   31.4

Circumference 5 (p. 44)
A.   25.12 cm   B.   15.7 ft.   C.   9 in.

Area of Circles 1 (p. 45)
A.   314   B.   28.26

Area of Circles 2 (p. 45)
A.   154   B. $314\frac{2}{7}$ C. $78\frac{4}{7}$

Area of Circles 3 (p. 45)
A.   78.5   B.   1,256
C.   Divide the circumference by 3.14 to find the diameter. Divide the diameter by 2 to find the radius. Square the radius and multiply by 3.14.
     A = 314 m²

Solid Figures 1 (p. 46)
A.   yes   B.   yes   C.   no   D.   yes
E.   yes

Solid Figures 2 (p. 46)
A.   6   B.   1   C.   6   D.   5
E.   2   F.   5   G.   4

Solid Figures 3 (p. 46)
A.   12 edges, 8 vertices
B.   8 edges, 5 vertices
C.   6 edges, 4 vertices
D.   9 edges, 6 vertices
E.   12 edges, 8 vertices
F.   15 edges, 10 vertices

Solid Figures 4 (p. 46)
A.   S   B.   A   C.   A   D.   N

Solid Figures 5 (p. 47)
A.   cylinder   B.   square pyramid
C.   rectangular prism   D.   cone

Solid Figures and Nets 1 (p. 47)
A.   cube   B.   square pyramid
C.   rectangular prism

Solid Figures and Nets 2 (p. 47)
A

Solid Figures and Nets 3 (p. 48)
A.   B.

Solid Figures and Nets 4 (p. 48)
Examples:

Surface Area of Rectangular Prisms 1 (p. 48)
384

Surface Area of Rectangular Prisms 2 (p. 48)
150 in.²

Surface Area of Rectangular Prisms 3 (p. 49)
126

Surface Area of Rectangular Prisms 4 (p. 49)
A.   126   B.   92   C.   96   D.   A

Surface Area of Rectangular Prisms 5 (p. 49)

Length of Side of Cube	Surface Area
1	6
2	24
4	96
8	384

The surface area becomes four times greater.

Volume of Rectangular Prisms 1 (p. 50)
80 cubes
Accept any reasonable explanation.
Example: I multiplied 4 x 4 and then multiplied
that by 5.

Volume of Rectangular Prisms 2 (p. 50)
A. 27   B. 125

Volume of Rectangular Prisms 3 (p. 50)
A. 21   B. 320

Volume of Rectangular Prisms 4 (p. 50)
Box A has the greater volume.
A. 210   B. 192

Volume of Rectangular Prisms 5 (p. 51)
A. 6 ft.   B. 4 cm   C. 8 in.^{3}

Volume of Triangular Prisms 1 (p. 51)
A. B = 3 in.^{2}, V = 18 in.^{3}
B. B = 32 in.^{2}, V = 224 in.^{3}

Volume of Triangular Prisms 2 (p. 51)
A. 70 in.^{3} B. 18 cm^2

Volume of Triangular Prisms 3 (p. 52)
B = 54 cm^2, V = 270 cm^3

Volume of Triangular Prisms 4 (p. 52)
B has the greater volume.
A. 96 cm^3 B. 120 cm^3

Volume of Cylinders 1 (p. 52)
A. B = 3.14 m^2, V = 18.84 m^3
B. B = 50.24 in.^{2}, V = 200.96 in.^{3}

Volume of Cylinders 2 (p. 53)
A. circle   B. area   C. height   D. cubic

Volume of Cylinders 3 (p. 53)
B has the greater volume.
A. B = 12.56 m^2, V = 75.36 m^3
B. B = 28.26 m^2, V = 113.04 m^3

Volume of Cylinders 4 (p. 53)
A. 3,140 cm^3 B. 785 cm^3

Volume of Cylinders 5 (p. 53)
A. 28.26 yd.^{2}
B. Accept any reasonable explanation.
     Example: I divided the volume by the height
     to get 28.26 square yards.

Ordered Pairs 1 (p. 54)
A. R   B. S   C. V   D. P

Ordered Pairs 2 (p. 54)
A (1, 4)   B (3, 0)   C (4, 5)   D (6, 2)

Ordered Pairs 3 (p. 54)
A. W   B. S   C. V   D. U

Ordered Pairs 4 (p. 54)
A. (-3, 1) B. (-2, -3) C. (1, 3)   D. (2, -2)

Lengths on the Coordinate Plane 1 (p. 55)
$\overline{AB}$ = 3 $\overline{CD}$ = 4 $\overline{EF}$ = 6

Lengths on the Coordinate Plane 2 (p. 55)
$\overline{JK}$ = 4 $\overline{LM}$ = 3 $\overline{NO}$ = 4

Lengths on the Coordinate Plane 3 (p. 55)
A (1, 6)   B (1, 1)   C (3, 1)   D (3, 3)
E (6, 3)   F (6, 6)
$\overline{AB}$ = 5 $\overline{AF}$ = 5 $\overline{CD}$ = 2 $\overline{EF}$ = 3
$\overline{DE}$ = 3 $\overline{BC}$ = 2